Dedicated to my best friend, Ben

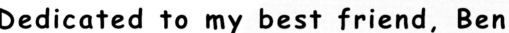

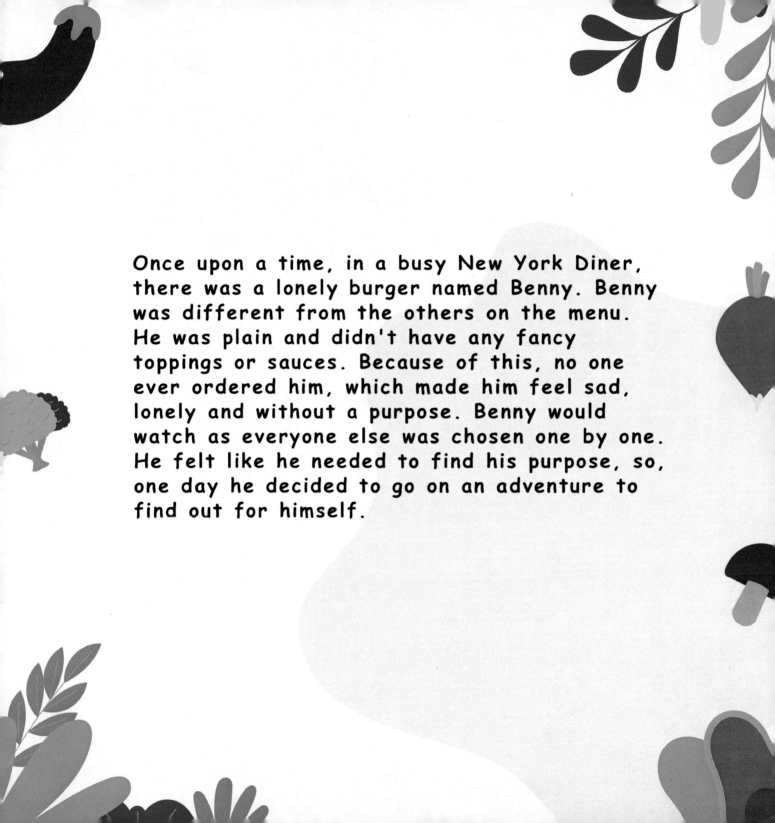

Once upon a time, in a busy New York Diner, there was a lonely burger named Benny. Benny was different from the others on the menu. He was plain and didn't have any fancy toppings or sauces. Because of this, no one ever ordered him, which made him feel sad, lonely and without a purpose. Benny would watch as everyone else was chosen one by one. He felt like he needed to find his purpose, so, one day he decided to go on an adventure to find out for himself.

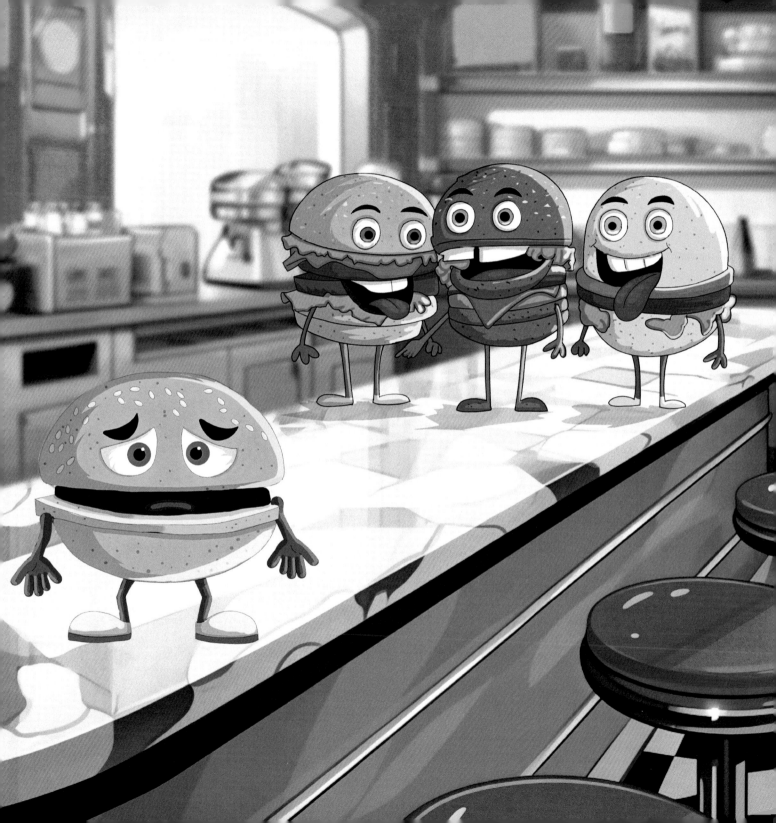

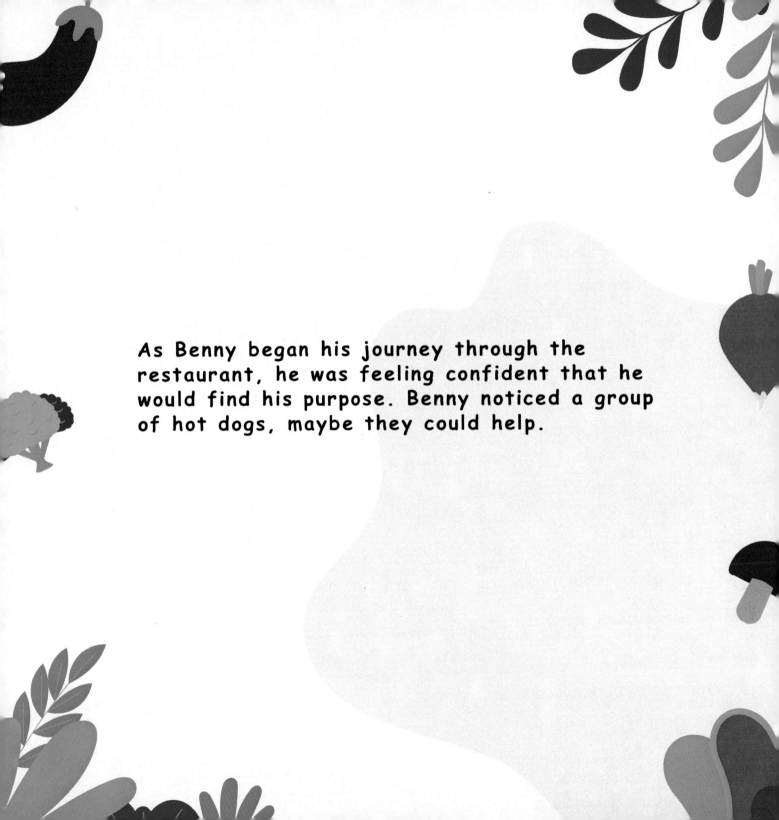

As Benny began his journey through the restaurant, he was feeling confident that he would find his purpose. Benny noticed a group of hot dogs, maybe they could help.

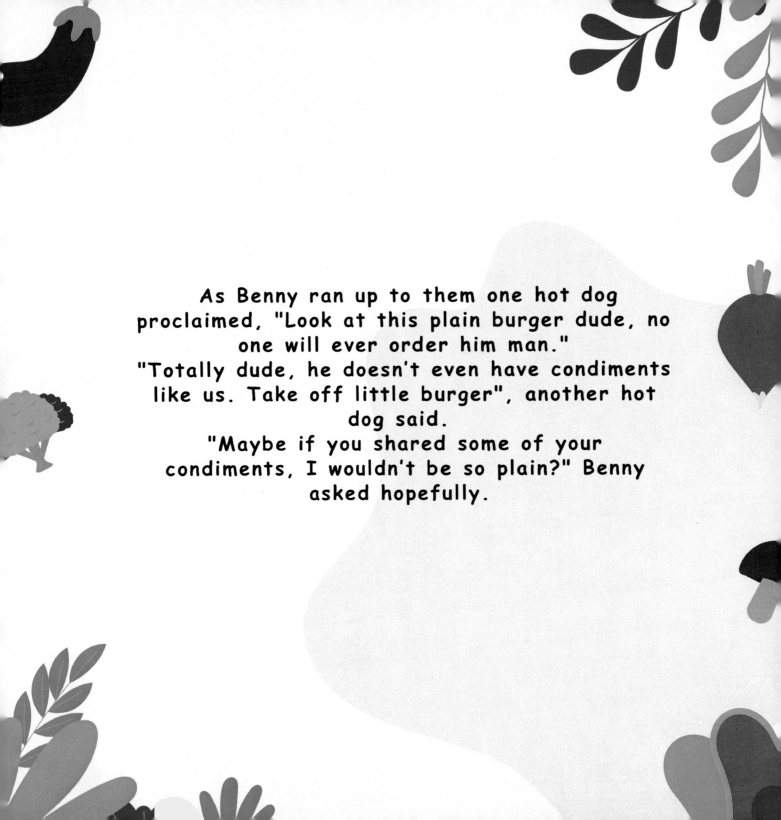

As Benny ran up to them one hot dog proclaimed, "Look at this plain burger dude, no one will ever order him man."
"Totally dude, he doesn't even have condiments like us. Take off little burger", another hot dog said.
"Maybe if you shared some of your condiments, I wouldn't be so plain?" Benny asked hopefully.

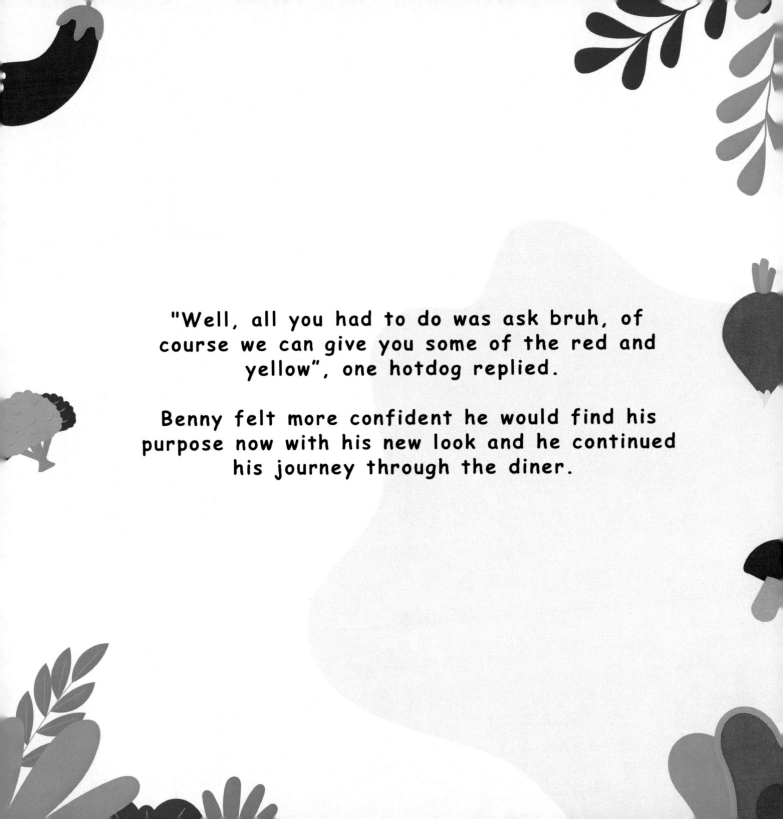

"Well, all you had to do was ask bruh, of course we can give you some of the red and yellow", one hotdog replied.

Benny felt more confident he would find his purpose now with his new look and he continued his journey through the diner.

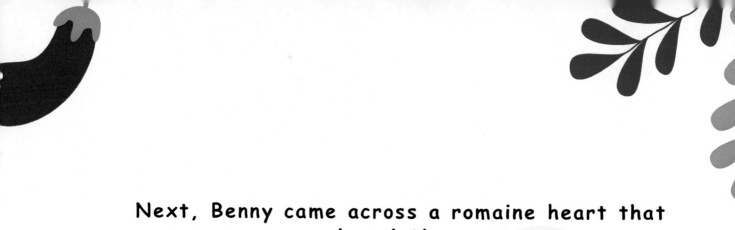

Next, Benny came across a romaine heart that is painting.

"Good day little burger! What a grand day to be expressing yourself through the wonderful art of painting! What brings you to this side of the restaurant?", Romania the romaine heart shouts.

"I was thinking if maybe I went on an adventure I could find my purpose. Earlier I met this group of hot dogs that gave me some ketchup and mustard and now I don't feel so plain. I am hoping you can give me a piece of your heart so I don't feel so ordinary", Benny replies.

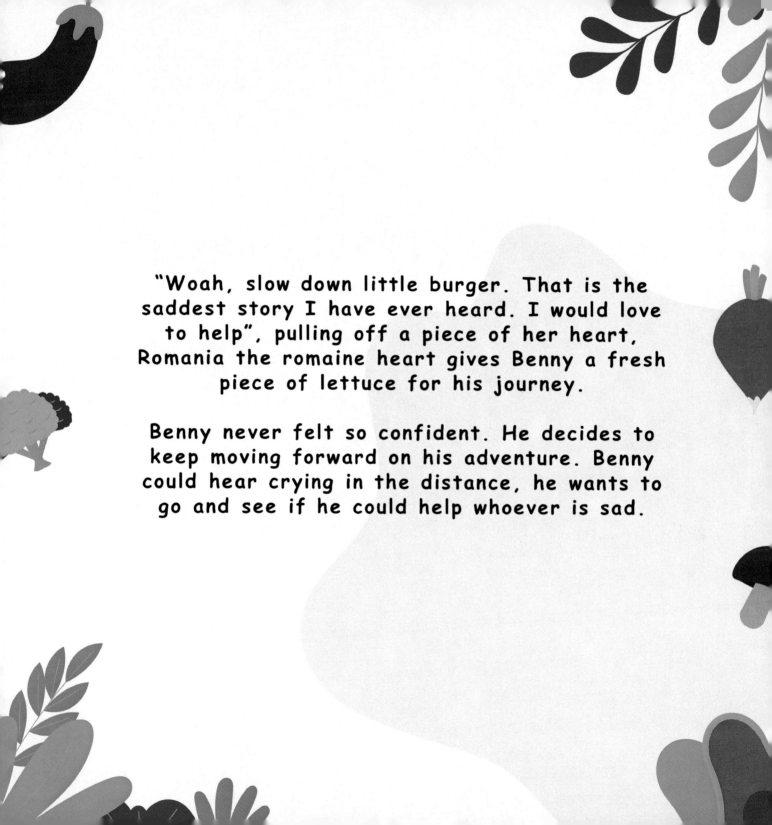

"Woah, slow down little burger. That is the saddest story I have ever heard. I would love to help", pulling off a piece of her heart, Romania the romaine heart gives Benny a fresh piece of lettuce for his journey.

Benny never felt so confident. He decides to keep moving forward on his adventure. Benny could hear crying in the distance, he wants to go and see if he could help whoever is sad.

Benny notices a crying onion sitting all alone.
"Why are you crying, Onion?"
Benny curiously asked.

"Because I only make people cry. No one is
everhappy when I open up",
Onion said sobbing.

"Well Onion, you could make me very happy by
sharing a ring or two with me"

"Really?" Onion said with excitement, "I would love to make someone happy for once!".

Onion swiftly tossed Benny 2 onion rings.

Benny was now feeling happier than ever. He couldn't help but feel like there was one last piece missing so, he continues his journey through the restaurant.

Benny finally came across a ripe tomato enjoying the sun.

"Excuse me Tomato, I don't mean to interrupt your sunbathing but I am here on an adventure to not be so plain. I think with the help of someone as fresh and juicy as you, I would be the perfect fit in the diner"

Benny proclaimed.

Taking off her sunglasses, the tomato looked at Benny smiling.

"Oh, honey you don't need my help. I think you're perfect and someone will choose you just the way you are. But, if you think it will help you on your adventure, then I would be glad to help", Tomato said confidently.

The juicy tomato passes over a couple of tomato slices and continues to bath in the sun uninterrupted.

Benny was finally starting to feel like he was just as special as the other burgers. He knew with his new toppings he wouldn't feel so plain. Benny decides to head back to the kitchen to show everyone his new look.

Upon returning to the kitchen Benny boasts about his new look, "Hey everyone, look! I am not so plain anymore. Do you…".

Benny was cut off by the sound of the bill printer:

ZZZZZZZZZZZZZZZZZzzzzzzzzzzzzzzz…

'PLAIN BURGER NO SAUCE',
The bill read.

Everyone sat back in disbelief. Never in their wildest dreams did they think a plain burger would be ordered.

Benny was shocked. Maybe Tomato was right, maybe he was fine just the way he was. It was then he realized that even though he used to be a plain burger without a purpose, he could still fulfill someone's life. No matter how plain he was, there would be someone who would want him just the way he is. In the moment, Benny knew he didn't need the fancy toppings that everyone else had, but that he was perfect just the way he had been. Benny is going to be just fine being a plain burger again.

THE END

Manufactured by Amazon.ca
Acheson, AB

11790291R00017